HIDE
AND DEFEND

HIDE AND DEFEND

By Kathleen N. Daly

Pictures by
Tim and Greg Hildebrandt

Golden Press · New York
Western Publishing Company, Inc.
Racine, Wisconsin

For wild animals, each day is a game of hide-and-seek. But it's a dangerous and serious game.

The danger comes when animals leave their nests and burrows and go to look for food. As they move about, they try to keep away from other creatures that might eat them.

Animals have many ways of hiding and of defending themselves. Sometimes the color of their coats help them to hide.

All the creatures on this page have brown fur or feathers during the short summer of the Arctic, where they live.

weasel

ptarmigan

collared lemming

Arctic fox

snowshoe hare

WINTER COATS

In the winter, fox and ermine, ptarmigan, snowshoe hare, and collared lemming are white as the snow around them. Their brown coats and feathers have slowly changed with the seasons. It is hard to see their new white coats against the snow.

Arctic fox

ptarmigan

ermine

collared lemming

snowshoe hare

The polar bear, huge and fearsome, is white all year round, and he seldom leaves the snowy white ice floes of the Far North.

STRIPES AND SPOTS

Which zebras are
harder to see

zebras in the jungle

or zebras in the zoo?

In a zoo, the black-and-white striped zebra stands out gaily
from its background. But in its natural home the stripes blend
well with the brilliant light and deep shadows of the trees
and tall grasses.

The stripes also help to break up the shape of the zebra.
From a distance it is hard to tell where the animal's head is,
or its legs.

SPEED HELPS, TOO

Many deer, antelope, and gazelles have spots and stripes, especially when they are young. These make it easier for the little animals to hide.

This baby deer, called a fawn, has white spots on its coat. When danger is near, it stays very still. The light and shade on its coat make it hard to see. Another thing that helps is that the fawn has no smell! And so the enemy cannot see it or smell it, and usually passes it by.

There are other animals that
are hard to see in the jungle.
The spots of the leopard and
the stripes of the orange-and-
black tiger help these animals
to fade into the background of
the trees and dry grass.

leopard

There are many kinds of antelope. Their delicate stripes blend well with the dappled light and shade of their homes.

Another protection of these animals is their speed. The pronghorn antelope can run 60 miles an hour, over short distances.

tiger

The eland is the biggest member of the antelope family.

WHICH IS WHICH?

There are many millions of insects in the world, far more than there are people. Yet we don't see them very often, for insects have many ways of hiding.

For example, many insects are colored green or brown, like the plants among which they live.

This butterfly, the kallima, looks like a dead leaf.

The inchworm can hold itself so stiffly that it looks just like a twig.

The glass-winged butterfly has see-through wings.

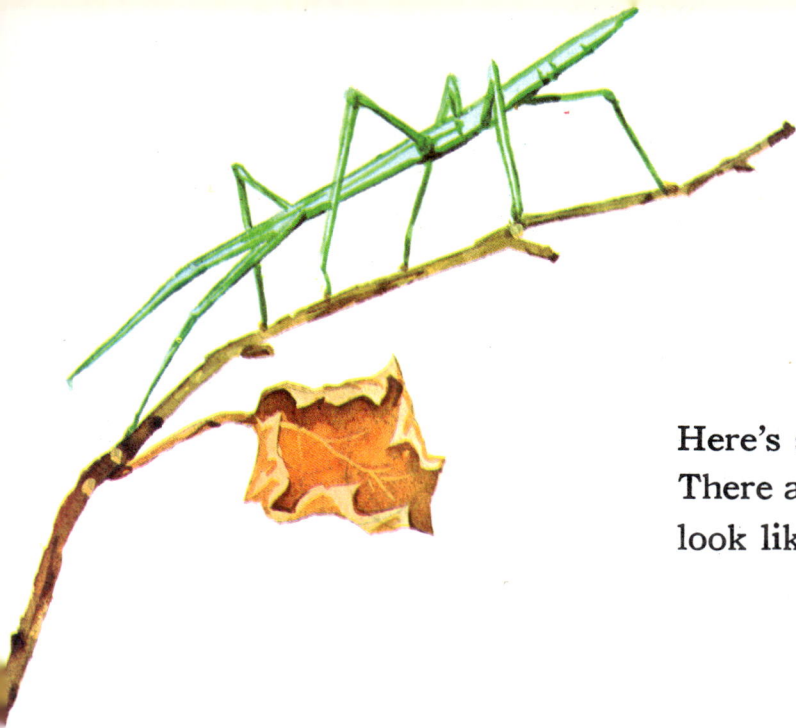

The walking stick looks like a stick—until it moves.

Here's something surprising! There are harmless insects that look like dangerous ones!

The gentle bee-fly looks like the stinging bumblebee.

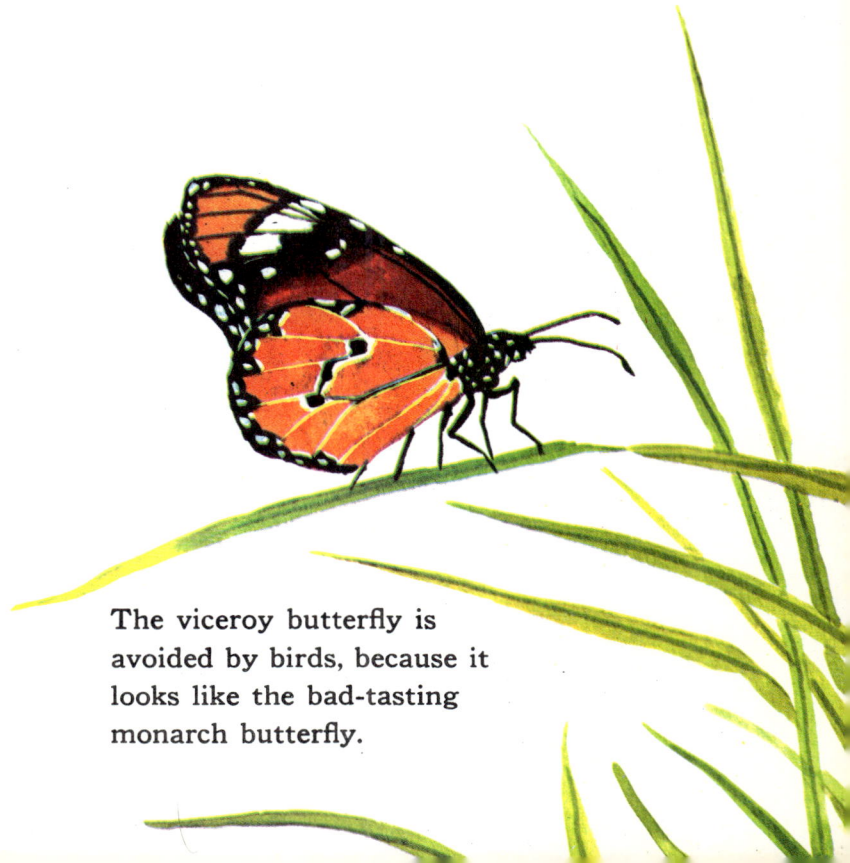

The viceroy butterfly is avoided by birds, because it looks like the bad-tasting monarch butterfly.

The porcupine fish can blow itself up into a big ball that is hard to swallow.

The sargassum fish is not easy to spot. Its knobs, tassels, frills, and streamers look exactly like the seaweeds of the Sargasso Sea, where it lives.

HIDING IN THE SEA

Ocean creatures, too, must protect themselves from other animals. They have many tricks that can fool even the most watchful hunters.

The flounder changes its speckles to match the sand or gravel of the sea bottom where it is resting.

The sponge crab cuts out a piece of sponge (which no fish will eat) and holds it over its back.

People think of octopuses and squids as great monsters of the deep. But many of them are small and very shy. They hide their soft bodies in underwater caves.

octopus

squid

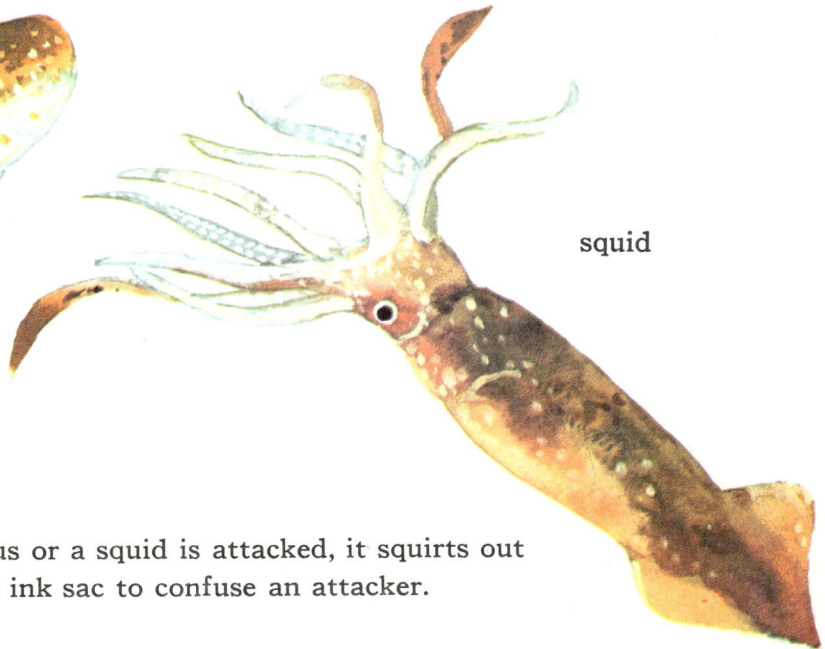

If an octopus or a squid is attacked, it squirts out ink from its ink sac to confuse an attacker.

ANIMALS THAT PLAY DEAD

Some animals, instead of running or hiding, "play possum" as the opossum does. This little animal is unusual in many ways. It rears its tiny babies in a pouch, like a kangaroo. When the babies are older, the mother carries them on her back.

When the opossum is attacked, it lies very still. Its enemy may think it is dead and leave it alone.

Some snakes and small animals "hide" by being very, very still. For example, rabbits, mice, and other small animals often sit quietly and do not move when danger is near.

The hog-nosed snake is another animal that plays dead. First, it puts on a very good show of being in pain. It twists and turns its long body as if it were hurt. Then it rolls over and lies still as if it had died.

A rabbit "freezing"

Some lizards pant, blow themselves up, and do little push-ups.

Other lizards show off their frilly collars and the crests on their backs, which makes them look big and scary.

Many lizards, when caught by their tail, can snap it off and then grow a new one.

Some lizards can change color.

Some shy snakes roll up in a ball.
The green whipsnake looks
like the vines in which it hides.

Cobras blow up great hoods
around their necks to make
themselves look bigger.

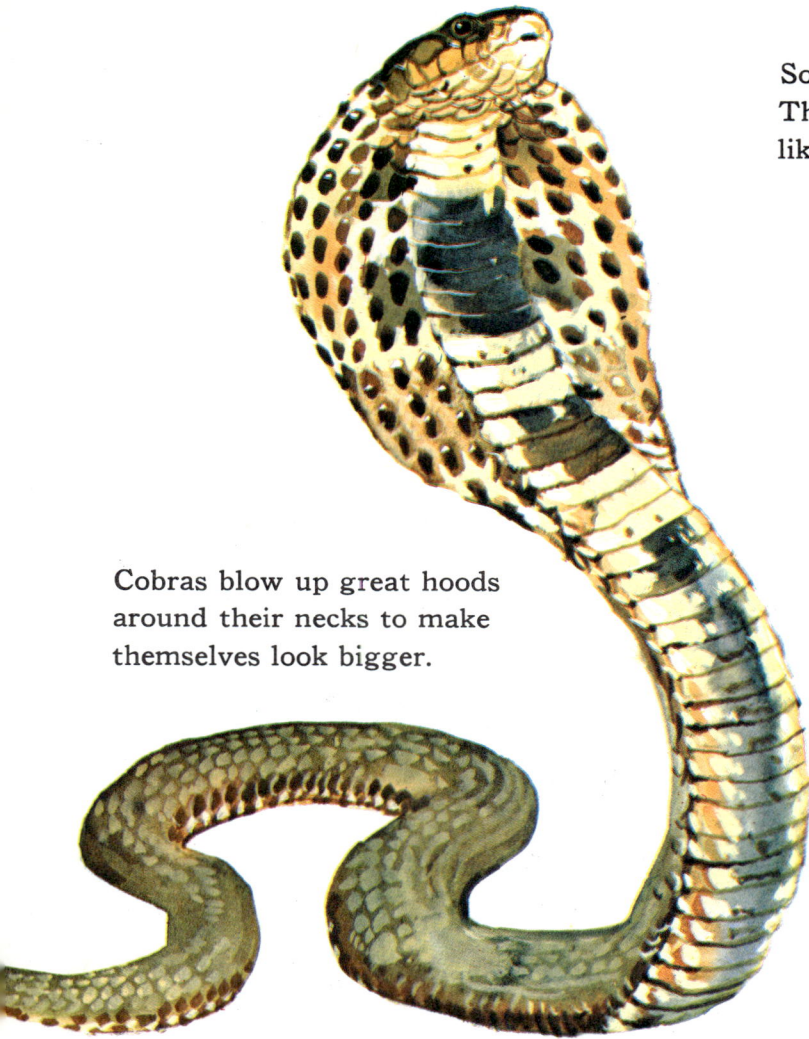

Some snakes dart into the
water to find safety.

SOME ANIMAL SHOW-OFFS

Snakes and lizards can be great show-offs when in danger.
They protect themselves with a number of tricks. Snakes
have especially clever ways of defending themselves.
Most of them hiss and sometimes spit.

ANIMALS IN ARMOR

Some animals, such as the turtle, have sturdy suits of armor. The turtle moves so slowly on its short legs that hunters can easily catch up with it. But then it pulls its head and legs into its shell, and there it hides.

The turtle's shell has a bottom and a top part. Even a sharp knife or a bear's strength can't pry that shell open. So the turtle is usually safe inside.

A turtle walking in the woods

The turtle safely inside its shell

The snail, too, has a shell on its back. It can pull its soft body into the shell and stay there, safe and snug.

Some armadillos have a jointed coat of armor. This one can roll itself into a tight ball so that nothing can get at its soft underbelly.

The pangolin, too, can roll into a ball. Its scales are very hard and sharp and can give bad cuts. That is why most animals leave it alone with its meal of ants.

HOW TO KEEP OTHERS AWAY

The skunk leads a peaceful life, for its neighbors seem to know about its scent spray. The skunk's striking black-and-white coat says, "Watch out!" If its attacker doesn't go away, the skunk turns its back and lifts its tail. Then out comes the spray, which stings the eyes and leaves a very bad smell.

A mother skunk with her babies. She protects the babies with a nasty-smelling spray.

Some other little animals use
their prickly coats to keep
strangers away.

Long, sharp spines on most of the porcupine's body
keep the animal safe. If the prickles stick into a soft
nose or mouth, they are hard to get out.

Another prickly animal is the little hedgehog.
It rolls itself into a ball, and most animals will
leave it alone.

SOME BIRD TRICKS

Birds are the most brilliantly colored creatures in nature. Often they live together in large flocks and help look after each other. Also, they move so fast that their enemies cannot catch them.

But a nesting bird must hide. Nearly always, the mother bird and her babies are speckled and dull in color. This makes them hard to spot.

If a hunter comes near the nest of a plover, the mother bird drags herself away as if she were wounded. She leads the enemy away from the nest.

The bittern, standing in the reeds, can look exactly like a cattail. The bird stretches its neck and sways in the breeze.

BUTTERFLIES AND MOTHS

Butterflies and moths have a number of ways of hiding. Many have showy "eye spots" that frighten their enemies. Some are as brightly colored as the flowers they feed upon. Some moths manage to look just like the tree barks upon which they rest.

One of the most perfect tree-bark disguises is that of the owlet moth. It settles itself so that its marks run exactly the same way as those of the tree.

From generation to generation, the peppered moth has even changed its color, for its home trees have become darker and darker with soot.

And so we see that right up to the present minute nature goes on changing to keep up with the times.